CW00749756

BOOK ANALYSIS

By Cosima Lumley

My Cousin Rachel

by Daphne du Maurier

Bright
≡Summaries.com

DAPHNE DU MAURIER

ENGLISH NOVELIST, SHORT-STORY WRITER AND PLAYWRIGHT

- **Born in London in 1907.**
- **Died in Cornwall in 1989.**
- **Notable works:**
  - *Rebecca* (1938), novel
  - *Jamaica Inn* (1936), novel
  - *The Birds* (1952), short story

Daphne du Maurier was a celebrated author and playwright who is known for her darkly gothic thrillers and romances. She was born in 1907 to the wealthy and prominent actor-manager Sir Gerald du Maurier (1873-1934) and the famous actress Muriel Beaumont (1876-1957). Brought up in Cornwall, she used her family connections to forge her career as a writer, publishing her first work, *The Loving Spirit* (1931), in her early twenties. The following year, in 1932, she married an officer in the British army, Sir Frederick Browning (1896-1965), with whom she had three children. Her literary career flourished, and in 1938 she published *Rebecca*, the story of a young bride haunted by memories of her husband's dead wife. This was an immediate hit; it sold nearly 3 million copies over the next 20 years and was adapted into both a play by du Maurier and a film by Alfred Hitchcock (English film director, 1899–1980). Hitchcock chose to direct not only *Rebecca*, but also the novel *Jamaica Inn* (1936) and her terrifying short story *The Birds* (1952). To date, du Maurier's literary works have spawned 13 film adaptations and over 40 television dramatisations, and they continue to be popular both as literary and cinematic pieces. Du Maurier died in 1989, aged 81, and was recognised for her contribution to the English canon in 1969 when she was made a Dame of the British Empire.

MY COUSIN RACHEL

A YOUNG MAN FALLS FOR THE COUSIN HE SUSPECTS OF MURDER

- **Genre:** novel
- **Reference edition:** du Maurier, D. (1981) *Four Great Cornish Novels: Jamaica Inn, Rebecca, Frenchman's Creek, My Cousin Rachel.* London: Victor Gollancz Ltd.
- **1st edition:** 1951
- **Themes:** love, illness, murder, marriage, women, the double, guilt, insanity

My Cousin Rachel centres on the relationship between the young and naïve Philip and his late cousin's enigmatic, older widow, Rachel. Initially, Philip suspects Rachel murdered his cousin, Ambrose; however, upon meeting her he falls in love with her and even transfers his inheritance, Ambrose's estate, to her. Afterwards, she refuses to marry him and when he falls ill he suspects she has poisoned him. While he is searching her rooms for incriminating items, Rachel steps onto an unstable bridge in the garden and plunges to her death. She is found by Phillip still calling for Ambrose.

Like du Maurier's earlier novel, *Rebecca*, *My Cousin Rachel* is a mystery romance which leaves its reader guessing till the very end, and even then, we are left unsure as to whether Rachel is the victim or the perpetrator. The story was inspired by a 17th-century portrait of Rachel Carew which du Maurier saw at Antony House, in Cornwall. The novel has spawned several adaptations, including Henry Koster's 1952 film starring Richard Burton, and more recently, Roger Mitchell's 2017 film starring Rachel Weisz and Sam Claflin.

SUMMARY

AMBROSE'S JOURNEY

The novel begins after Rachel's death, as Phillip considers the events leading up to her death. His reflections on the past, and his consequential guilt, lead him to tell the story of his and Rachel's tragic romance. He narrates how, as an orphan, he was brought up by his cousin Ambrose Ashley, a bachelor who was mistrustful of women and raised Phillip in an entirely male household, making Phillip naïve and inexperienced when it came to women. The story begins with Ambrose leaving his damp Cornish home due to his ill-health and travelling to Florence, in Italy. The 23-year-old Phillip is left behind, and hears of his cousin's escapades in Italy intermittently by letter. He learns that his cousin has met and married a charming Italian woman called Rachel, the widowed Contessa Sangalletti. However, following the marriage Ambrose becomes ill again, and he writes to Phillip implying his wife is poisoning him and eventually pleading with him to come and rescue him.

AN UNSUCCESSFUL RESCUE

Upon hearing of Ambrose's plight, Phillip travels to Italy immediately. However, upon his arrival he finds that his cousin has died and that Rachel has left Villa Sangaletti, where they were staying. Although he is informed that Ambrose died of a brain tumour, Phillip suspects Rachel has murdered him, and swears he will avenge Ambrose. When he returns to Ambrose's estate in Cornwall, he is told by his godfather and now guardian, Nick Kendall, that he will gain control of his inheritance, Ambrose's estate, on his 25th birthday. He is also informed that Rachel has arrived in Plymouth in order to deliver Ambrose's belongings, and Philip insists that she come stay at Ambrose's estate so that he can confront her. He confides his suspicions to Louise, Nick's daughter. However, when Rachel arrives Philip is surprised to find her petite and pretty rather than the monstrous, murderous figure he had imagined. They bond over their shared love of gardening, and Philip asks her not to return to Italy and stay with him instead.

THE CHRISTMAS PARTY

With Rachel's help, Philip decides to celebrate Christmas by throwing a big party on the estate for all the tenants, as Ambrose used to do. He also decides to gift his tenants Ambrose's old clothes and give Rachel a family heirloom, a pearl collar traditionally worn by the Ashley women on their wedding days. That night, Rachel kisses Philip, encouraging his affections. However, upon seeing the family necklace on Rachel, Nick Kendall, Philip's guardian who is in control of his wealth as he is yet to turn 25, reprimands him for this and tells him he has no right to gift the Ambrose family possessions. Philip is furious; however, Rachel covers for him, saying he had only lent it to her for the Christmas party and she fully intended to return it.

AN UNSAVOURY LETTER

Meanwhile, one of the tenants discovers a letter in one of Ambrose's old items of clothing, which he had been gifted at the Christmas party. He hands it over to Philip, who discovers in its contents that Rachel had miscarried a child. The letter also relates Ambrose's suspicions about the relationship between Rachel and her Italian confidante Reinaldi, with whom he believed she was having an affair. Additionally, he criticised her extravagant spending. It is revealed that Ambrose had drawn up a will which left the entirety of his estate to Rachel; however, he had left it unsigned due to his suspicions. Due to this discovery, Philip asks his attorney to transfer Ambrose's estate to Rachel when he turns 25, believing this to be the right thing to do. However, upon his attorney's insistence, he adds a clause stating that the estate will return to him if she ever marries. When he returns home, Reinaldi is there with Rachel. Reinaldi patronises and insults Philip and excludes him from conversation by speaking in Italian, making Philip resentful and suspicious of him.

THE BIRTHDAY

On his 25th birthday, Philip climbs up through Rachel's bedroom window at night carrying all the family jewels in a satchel, which he hands over to her saying they now belong to her. They make love that night, and Philip believes that Rachel intends to marry him despite the fact that a formal proposal has not been made. The following day Rachel goes to see Nick Kendall to check the legality of the estate document, and is assured of its contents. During dinner with the Kendalls, Philip announces his engagement to Rachel, much to her astonishment; she denies that there is such an engagement and tells Philip that she does not intend to marry him. Drunk and furious at this, Philip places his hands around Rachel's neck and begs her to marry him. She runs from him, and locks herself in her room.

THE SUSPICIOUS ILLNESS

After this Philip becomes ill and delirious with headaches. He wakes up weeks later to find Rachel sitting beside him. He remembers Rachel nursing him over the past weeks, giving him strange concoctions to drink, and he suspects that she is poisoning him as she poisoned Ambrose. He finds out that Reinaldi has been in England and that Rachel has slipped off to see him every once in a while. This deepens his suspicions, and he begins to believe that Rachel has a dark side which she is in thrall to and that he must therefore save her from her own evil nature.

THE BRIDGE

Upon his return from church, the foreman tells Phillip that the bridge of the veranda is being repaired and should not be walked on since it will not bear any weight. The Kendalls come for dinner that night and Philip asks Louise to stay with him so that he can share his suspicions about Rachel and so they can search her rooms for incriminating items. Rachel meanwhile tells Philip that she is going for a walk on the veranda, and after considering the matter, Philip decides not to tell her about the bridge. Louise and Philip find no evidence of poisoning or wrongdoing in Rachel's rooms, and Philip rushes out onto the veranda to stop Rachel from falling to her death, realising he may have misjudged her. However, it is too late and Philip finds Rachel's limp and broken body, which he cradles in his arms. With her final breath she looks up at him and calls him Ambrose.

CHARACTER STUDY

RACHEL ASHLEY

Rachel Ashley is the enigmatic anti-heroine of the novel. She is described as short and feminine, with small hands and fine eyes, a good sense of humour and remarkable intelligence. Born to an English father and Italian mother, she is brought up in Italy where she marries an Italian nobleman, Count Sangalletti. However, when Sangalletti is killed in a duel he leaves Rachel childless and in excessive debt. She then meets Ambrose at the mature age of 35 and they bond over a shared love of gardening before getting married. However, Ambrose quickly becomes suspicious that she is poisoning him and is plotting his demise with the help of the doctors and her Italian friend, Reinaldi. Later, after Ambrose's death, Philip also falls in love with her. However, like Ambrose, he suspects her of poisoning him and so he lets her fall to her death on an unstable bridge. Du Maurier never dispels the uncertainty around Rachel, and like Philip, the haunting doubt, "Was Rachel innocent or guilty?" (p. 633) plagues us throughout the narrative. Her identity is in constant flux, as shown in Philip's many re-imaginings of her as a "bitter creature, crabbed and old", "a larger Mrs Pascoe, loud-voiced, arrogant", "a petulant spoilt doll, with corkscrew curls" or "a viper, sinuous and silent" (p. 685). These ambiguities are emphasised the fact this is a first-person narrative and therefore we are limited to the somewhat unreliable eyes of Philip. Rachel's multiple identities symbolise the multiplicity of female stereotypes, from the damsel in distress, to the femme fatale, and even to the witch with her many tisana brews. She becomes the threatening female presence in the all-male world of Ambrose, and it is apt, therefore, that she perishes in this masculine world.

PHILIP ASHLEY

Philip Ashley is the first-person narrator of *My Cousin Rachel*, and it is through his eyes that we see the tragic events of the story unfold. Philip is modelled on his cousin and guardian Ambrose, who is his idol and sole father-figure, having been orphaned at 18 months. Philip is Ambrose's doppelganger: "I have become so like him I might be his ghost. My eyes are his eyes" (p. 633). Their identities are blurred throughout the text, "he lived again in me, repeating his own mistakes" (*ibid*.), as Philip falls for the same woman, Rachel, and similarly suspects she is poisoning him. Du Maurier often describes their personalities in tandem: "We were dreamers, both of us, unpractical, reserved, full of great theories never put to the test, and like all dreamers, asleep to the waking world" (p. 634). Having grown up with no mother or female influence of any kind he carries the same mistrust and stereotypical views of women as his cousin, Ambrose. He himself has a very masculine figure with "big feet and arms and legs, sprawling and angular" (*ibid*.), the opposite of Rachel's diminutive appearance. The story is recounted by Philip after the events of the novel have happened, and from the outset he is plagued by guilt over Rachel's death, in which he played a role since he wilfully let her walk into danger. As a first-person narrator Philip is somewhat unreliable, especially since his views on Rachel and his intentions with her are constantly changing, meaning that the reader has to carefully select what is truth from what is prejudice. However, like Philip, the reader is left doubting whether Philip is the hero of the story, or if he is its true villain, having let an innocent woman die due to his own insecurities.

AMBROSE ASHLEY

Ambrose Ashley is the narrator Philip Ashley's older cousin and guardian. When Philip's parents die, leaving him orphaned at the age of 18 months, Ambrose takes pity on the child and decides to raise him as his own. Philip looks up to Ambrose as his "guardian, father, brother, counsellor, as in fact, [his] whole world" (p. 631), and "the whole object of [his] life is to resemble him" (p. 632). Ambrose is pictured as "stooping" with "long arms, [...] rather clumsy looking hands" and a "sudden smile" (p. 633). He is described as a "shy", "eccentric" and "unorthodox" (p. 636) man who is "mistrustful" (*ibid.*) of women and banishes all female influences, such as Philip's nanny, from the house. He even describes himself as "a crusty cynical woman hater" (p. 638). However, when he meets Rachel, with whom he shares a love of gardening, he falls in love and marries her. As he falls ill he becomes suspicious of Rachel, and writes to Philip about his insecurities. While it is revealed that Ambrose dies of a brain tumour, like his father, some doubt is left in the minds of the reader and Philip as to whether or not this is truly the case. Within the text, Ambrose and Philip are seen as doppelgangers of each other, not only do they resemble each other ("my features are his features", p. 633), but they also are doomed to repeat each other's actions.

NICK KENDALL

Nick Kendall is Philip's godfather, and after Ambrose's death he becomes his legal guardian who has control over Ambrose's estate until Philip turns 25. He is the voice of reason in the story with his "plain, straightforward way" (p. 634) of speaking. He is level-headed and rational, unlike Philip, whom he often reprimands for being driven by an excess of feeling. For example, he warns Philip not to transfer all his possessions to Rachel and not to be blinded by his love for her. The two confront each other after Philip gifts Rachel a pearl necklace which is a family heirloom, and while Nick is an old family friend, the relationship between Nick and Philip is often complex and resentful.

ANALYSIS

WOMEN AND SEXUALITY IN *MY COUSIN RACHEL*

Published in 1951, *My Cousin Rachel* is a subtle exploration of women and the patriarchal model of womanhood in mid-20th-century society. It is no accident that the sexually experienced and autonomous Rachel is viewed from the perspective of male fear and inexperience in the form of Philip Ashley's first-person narration. The obsession with gender roles and their separation is obvious from the outset of the novel, as the mistrustful Ambrose banishes all female influence from his Cornish home and raises Philip with his misogynistic views of women.

Philip echoes his guardian's views when he imagines Rachel, before he meets her, as a spinster ("a bitter creature, crabbed and old", p. 685), a silly girl ("a petulant spoilt doll", *ibid.*) or a dehumanised threat ("a viper, sinuous and silent", *ibid.*). She belongs to the sensuous world of Italy, exotic and different. Philip's doubt as to whether she is innocent or guilty reflects the polarised patriarchal perspective of women as the innocent virgin or the guilty temptress. It is no coincidence that Philip begins to believe that she is guilty only after his 25th birthday when she has sex with him, and yet refuses to marry him, as is socially expected. The fact that Rachel is sterile following a miscarriage means sex for her is purely for pleasure, rather than a means of re-production, as society dictates. The fact that he is unable to control her, as she is an autonomous woman of means, having received Ambrose's estate, transforms her into a threat. A fear of female independence and sexuality permeates the text, and even the title "My Cousin Rachel" is an attempt by Philip to finally own the woman who always eluded him.

Du Maurier's deft exploration of female sexuality and its ambiguities could be seen to be rooted in her own ambiguous sexuality. While she was married to a British army officer, it is likely she had lesbian affairs and it is known that she fell for several women, including the glamourous Ellen Doubleday (1899-1978), who was the wife of her publisher. Several letters reveal her intense and unrequited love for this woman, who it is thought was the inspiration for Rachel. In fact, similar to her juxtaposition of Italy and Cornwall in the novel to represent the male and female worlds, she often referred to her heterosexual encounters as "Cairo" and to her homosexual encounters as "Venice" in her letters. Her father also often spoke about du Maurier's wish that she had been born a boy (Thorpe, 2007). It is clear that just as Rachel is constrained and villainised for her open sexuality and autonomy in the text, du Maurier felt some form of entrapment as a woman wishing for the freedom of being a man in a patriarchal world.

DU MAURIER'S USE OF THE DOUBLE IN *MY COUSIN RACHEL*

Du Maurier uses the classic gothic device of the double in *My Cousin Rachel* to heighten the eerie suspense of the text. The most significant double of the text is that of the protagonist, Philip Ashley, and his long-term guardian Ambrose. These two not only resemble each other physically, to the point that Philip "might be [Ambrose's] ghost" (p. 633), but Philip also repeats his cousin's actions almost to the letter. He, like Ambrose, is inexperienced in the world of women, but falls for Rachel; he too adores her and wishes to marry her, and then subsequently turns on her, believing her to be poisoning him. As Philip states at the beginning of the novel, "he lived again in me, repeating his own mistakes, [he] caught the disease once more" (*ibid.*). Du Maurier's deft use of the double turns Ambrose into a ghostly presence throughout the text, as his cousin animates him and gives him life. It is clear also, for example, that Rachel sees her husband, Ambrose, in Philip, and it is suggested that this is part of her attraction to him; "It was not I she saw, but Ambrose. Not Philip, but a phantom" (p. 634). Their identities are blurred throughout the text, and it is therefore unsurprising that Rachel's last words addressed to Philip are "Ambrose" (p. 847).

Du Maurier's deft use of the double is a gothic archetype, as can be seen in classic gothic texts of the late 19th century, including Robert Louis Stevenson's (Scottish writer, 1850-1894) *The Curious Case of Dr Jekyll and Mr. Hyde* (1886) and Oscar Wilde's (Irish writer, 1854-1900) *The Picture of Dorian Gray* (1890). While the use of doubling had lost popularity in the 20th century, du Maurier brings it back to brilliant effect, not only in *My Cousin Rachel,* but also in her earlier texts including *The Scapegoat* (1957) in which an Englishman, John, lives out the life of his own French double, Jean, a lively and disreputable Frenchman. In fact, du Maurier herself had a double; she invented a male alter ego called Eric Avon, who lived out her own fantasies of being a boy with greater freedom, more daring and adventure than she ever could have as a woman. In a letter to Maureen Baker-Munton, dated 4 July 1957, du Maurier explains her use of the double:

> "We [du Maurier and her husband] are both doubles. So is everyone. Every one of us has his, or her, dark side. Which is to overcome the other? This is the purpose of the book [*The Scapegoat*]. And it ends, as you know, with the problem unsolved, except that the suggestion there, when I finished it, was that the two sides of the man's nature had to fuse together to give birth to a third, well balanced. Know Thyself." (Buzwell, 2016)

However, it is perhaps Rachel's dual and contra-dictory role within the text as the poisoner and the loving woman who nurses Philip back to health, which is the most interesting use of dou-bling. Just as there are two ways of interpreting Rachel's actions, Philip too could be seen either as a killer, allowing his innocent cousin to fall to her death, or a just avenger of Ambrose's death. By leaving these aspects of the text unresolved, du Maurier demonstrates that often the charac-terisation of a person is not cut and dry; it is not a simple question of who is innocent and who is guilty. It seems that everyone in *My Cousin Rachel* is guilty in some form or another. As du Maurier puts it in her letter, "Every one of us has his, or her, dark side", and this is the double that haunts us.

FURTHER REFLECTION

SOME QUESTIONS TO THINK ABOUT...

- "Was Rachel innocent or guilty?" (p. 633). Who is the true villain of *My Cousin Rachel?*
- Discuss du Maurier's use of setting, particularly the contrast between Florence and Cornwall, within *My Cousin Rachel*.
- To what extent is Philip Ashley an unreliable narrator in *My Cousin Rachel?*
- Discuss the theme of possession in *My Cousin Rachel*.
- Discuss how Alfred Hitchcock's 1952 film adaptation and Roger Michell's 2017 adaptation of *My Cousin Rachel* differ in their presentation of Rachel.
- Discuss whether or not *My Cousin Rachel* can be seen as a feminist narrative about female emancipation.
- "See what a moment of passion can bring upon a fellow" (p.631). To what extent are both Ambrose and Philip a victim of their own emotions?

We want to hear from you!
Leave a comment on your online library
and share your favourite books on social media!

FURTHER READING

REFERENCE EDITION

- du Maurier, D. (1981) *Four Great Cornish Novels: Jamaica Inn, Rebecca, Frenchman's Creek, My Cousin Rachel*. London: Victor Gollancz Ltd.

REFERENCE STUDIES

- Buzwell, G. (2016) Discovering Literature: 20th Century. *British Library*. [Online]. [Accessed 14 December 2018]. Available from: <https://www.bl.uk/20th-century-literature/articles/daphne-du-maurier-and-the-gothic-tradition>

- Thorpe, V. (2007) Du Maurier's lesbian loves on film. *The Guardian*. [Online]. [Accessed 14 December 2018]. Available from: <https://www.theguardian.com/uk/2007/feb/11/books.media>

ADAPTATIONS

- *My Cousin Rachel*. (1952) [Film]. Alfred Hitchcock. Dir. USA: 20th Century Fox.

- *My Cousin Rachel*. (2017) [Film]. Roger Mitchell. Dir. UK/USA: Fox Searchlight Pictures.

MORE FROM
BRIGHTSUMMARIES.COM

- Reading guide – *Jamaica Inn* by Daphne du Maurier.
- Reading guide – *Rebecca* by Daphne du Maurier.
- Reading guide – *The Birds* by Daphne du Maurier.

Although the editor makes every effort to
verify the accuracy of the information published,
BrightSummaries.com accepts no responsibility for
the content of this book.

www.brightsummaries.com

Ebook EAN: 9782808017169

Paperback EAN: 9782808017176

Legal Deposit: D/2019/12603/25

Cover: © Primento

Digital conception by Primento, the digital partner of
publishers.

Printed by Amazon Italia Logistica S.r.l.
Torrazza Piemonte (TO), Italy

12961301R00030